LYSISTRATA

By ARISTOPHANES

Lysistrata
By Aristophanes
Translated by The Athenian Society

Print ISBN 13: 978-1-4209-5867-6
eBook ISBN 13: 978-1-4209-5868-3

Cover Image: a detail of on illustration by Jean de Bosschere from "The Eleven Comedies" by Aristophanes, published by Horace Liveright, New York, 1928.

Please visit *www.digireads.com*

CONTENTS

Introduction

The 'Lysistrata,' the third and concluding play of the War and Peace series, was not produced till ten years later than its predecessor, the 'Peace,' viz. in 411 B.C. It is now the twenty-first year of the War, and there seems as little prospect of peace as ever. A desperate state of things demands a desperate remedy, and the Poet proceeds to suggest a burlesque solution of the difficulty.

The women of Athens, led by Lysistrata and supported by female delegates from the other states of Hellas, determine to take matters into their own hands and force the men to stop the War. They meet in solemn conclave, and Lysistrata expounds her scheme, the rigorous application to husbands and lovers of a self-denying ordinance—"we must refrain from the male organ altogether." Every wife and mistress is to refuse all sexual favours whatsoever, till the men have come to terms of peace. In cases where the women *must* yield 'par force majeure,' then it is to be with an ill grace and in such a way as to afford the minimum of gratification to their partner; they are to lie passive and take no more part in the amorous game than they are absolutely obliged to. By these means Lysistrata assures them they will very soon gain their end. "If we sit indoors prettily dressed out in our best transparent silks and prettiest gewgaws, and with our 'mottes' all nicely depilated, their tools will stand up so stiff that they will be able to deny us nothing." Such is the burden of her advice.

After no little demur, this plan of campaign is adopted, and the assembled women take a solemn oath to observe the compact faithfully. Meantime as a precautionary measure they seize the Acropolis, where the State treasure is kept; the old men of the city assault the doors, but are repulsed by "the terrible regiment" of women. Before long the device of the bold Lysistrata proves entirely effective, Peace is concluded, and the play ends with the hilarious festivities of the ATHENIAN and Spartan plenipotentiaries in celebration of the event.

This drama has a double Chorus—of women and of old men, and much excellent fooling is got out of the fight for possession of the citadel between the two hostile bands; while the broad jokes and decidedly suggestive situations arising out of the general idea of the plot outlined above may be "better imagined than described."

Dramatis Personae

LYSISTRATA
CALONICÉ
MYRRHINÉ
LAMPITO
STRATYLLIS
A MAGISTRATE
CINESIAS. A CHILD
HEARLD OF THE LACEDAEMONIANS
ENVOYS OF THE LACEDAEMONIANS
POLYCHARIDES
MARKET LOUNGERS
A SERVANT
AN ATHENIAN CITIZEN
CHORUS OF OLD MEN
CHORUS OF WOMEN

SCENE: In a public square at Athens; afterwards before the gates of the Acropolis, and finally within the precincts of the citadel.

Lysistrata

LYSISTRATA. [*Alone.*] Ah! if only they had been invited to a Bacchic revelling, or a feast of Pan or Aphrodité or Genetyllis,[1] why! the streets would have been impassable for the thronging tambourines! Now there's never a woman here—ah! except my neighbour Calonicé, whom I see approaching yonder.... Good day, Calonicé.

CALONICÉ. Good day, Lysistrata; but pray, why this dark, forbidding face, my dear? Believe me, you don't look a bit pretty with those black lowering brows.

LYSISTRATA. Oh! Calonicé, my heart is on fire; I blush for our sex. Men *will* have it we are tricky and sly....

CALONICÉ. And they are quite right, upon my word!

LYSISTRATA. Yet, look you, when the women are summoned to meet for a matter of the last importance, they lie abed instead of coming.

CALONICÉ. Oh! they will come, my dear; but 'tis not easy, you know, for women to leave the house. One is busy pottering about her husband; another is getting the servant up; a third is putting her child asleep, or washing the brat or feeding it.

LYSISTRATA. But I tell you, the business that calls them here is far and away more urgent.

CALONICÉ. And why *do* you summon us, dear Lysistrata? What is it all about?

LYSISTRATA. About a big affair.[2]

CALONICÉ. And is it thick too?

LYSISTRATA. Yes indeed, both big and great.

CALONICÉ. And we are not all on the spot!

LYSISTRATA. Oh! if it were what you suppose, there would be never an absentee. No, no, it concerns a thing I have turned about and about this way and that of many sleepless nights.

---

[1] At Athens more than anywhere the festivals of Bacchus (Dionysus) were celebrated with the utmost pomp—and also with the utmost licence, not to say licentiousness.

Pan—the rustic god and king of the Satyrs; his feast was similarly an occasion of much coarse self-indulgence.

Aphrodité Colias—under this name the goddess was invoked by courtesans as patroness of sensual, physical love. She had a temple on the promontory of Colias, on the Attic coast—whence the surname.

The Genetyllides were minor deities, presiding over the act of generation, as the name indicates. Dogs were offered in sacrifice to them—presumably because of the lubricity of that animal.

At the festivals of Dionysus, Pan and Aphrodité women used to perform lascivious dances to the accompaniment of the beating of tambourines. Lysistrata implies that the women she had summoned to council cared really for nothing but wanton pleasures.

[2] An obscene *double entendre*; Calonicé understands, or pretends to understand, Lysistrata as meaning a long and thick "membrum virile"!

CALONICÉ. It must be something mighty fine and subtle for you to have turned it about so!

LYSISTRATA. So fine, it means just this, Greece saved by the women!

CALONICÉ. By women! Why, its salvation hangs on a poor thread then!

LYSISTRATA. Our country's fortunes depend on us—it is with us to undo utterly the Peloponnesians.

CALONICÉ. That would be a noble deed truly!

LYSISTRATA. To exterminate the Boeotians to a man!

CALONICÉ. But surely you would spare the eels.[3]

LYSISTRATA. For Athens' sake I will never threaten so fell a doom; trust me for that. However, if the Boeotian and Peloponnesian women join us, Greece is saved.

CALONICÉ. But how should women perform so wise and glorious an achievement, we women who dwell in the retirement of the household, clad in diaphanous garments of yellow silk and long flowing gowns, decked out with flowers and shod with dainty little slippers?

LYSISTRATA. Nay, but those are the very sheet-anchors of our salvation—those yellow tunics, those scents and slippers, those cosmetics and transparent robes.

CALONICÉ. How so, pray?

LYSISTRATA. There is not a man will wield a lance against another …

CALONICÉ. Quick, I will get me a yellow tunic from the dyer's.

LYSISTRATA. … or want a shield.

CALONICÉ. I'll run and put on a flowing gown.

LYSISTRATA. … or draw a sword.

CALONICÉ. I'll haste and buy a pair of slippers this instant.

LYSISTRATA. Now tell me, would not the women have done best to come?

CALONICÉ. Why, they should have *flown* here!

LYSISTRATA. Ah! my dear, you'll see that like true Athenians, they will do everything too late.[4] … Why, there's not a woman come from the shoreward parts, not one from Salamis.[5]

CALONICÉ. But I know for certain they embarked at daybreak.

LYSISTRATA. And the dames from Acharnae![6] why, I thought they would have been the very first to arrive.

---

[3] The eels from Lake Copaïs in Boeotia were esteemed highly by epicures.

[4] This is the reproach Demosthenes constantly levelled against his ATHENIAN fellow-countrymen—their failure to seize opportunity.

[5] An island of the Saronic Gulf, lying between Magara and Attica. It was separated by a narrow strait—scene of the naval battle of Salamis, in which the Athenians defeated Xerxes—only from the Attic coast, and was subject to Athens.

[6] A deme, or township, of Attica, lying five or six miles north of Athens. The Acharnians were throughout the most extreme partisans of the warlike party during the Peloponnesian struggle. See 'The Acharnians.'

CALONICÉ. Theagenes wife[7] at any rate is sure to come; she has actually been to consult Hecaté.... But look! here are some arrivals—and there are more behind. Ah! ha! now what countrywomen may they be?

LYSISTRATA. They are from Anagyra.[8]

CALONICÉ. Yes! upon my word, 'tis a levy *en masse* of all the female population of Anagyra!

MYRRHINÉ. Are we late, Lysistrata? Tell us, pray; what, not a word?

LYSISTRATA. I cannot say much for you, Myrrhiné! you have not bestirred yourself overmuch for an affair of such urgency.

MYRRHINÉ. I could not find my girdle in the dark. However, if the matter is so pressing, here we are; so speak.

LYSISTRATA. No, but let us wait a moment more, till the women of Boeotia arrive and those from the Peloponnese.

MYRRHINÉ. Yes, that is best.... Ah! here comes Lampito.

LYSISTRATA. Good day, Lampito, dear friend from Lacedaemon. How well and handsome you look! what a rosy complexion! and how strong you seem; why, you could strangle a bull surely!

LAMPITO. Yes, indeed, I really think I could. 'Tis because I do gymnastics and practise the kick dance.[9]

LYSISTRATA. And what superb bosoms!

LAMPITO. La! you are feeling me as if I were a beast for sacrifice.

LYSISTRATA. And this young woman, what countrywoman is she?

LAMPITO. She is a noble lady from Boeotia.

LYSISTRATA. Ah! my pretty Boeotian friend, you are as blooming as a garden.

CALONICÉ. Yes, on my word! and the garden is so prettily weeded too![10]

LYSISTRATA. And who is this?

LAMPITO. 'Tis an honest woman, by my faith! she comes from Corinth.

LYSISTRATA. Oh! honest, no doubt then—as honesty goes at Corinth.[11]

LAMPITO. But who has called together this council of women, pray?

[7] The precise reference is uncertain, and where the joke exactly comes in. The Scholiast says Theagenes was a rich, miserly and superstitious citizen, who never undertook any enterprise without first consulting an image of Hecaté, the distributor of honour and wealth according to popular belief; and his wife would naturally follow her husband's example.

[8] A deme of Attica, a small and insignificant community—a 'Little Pedlington' in fact.

[9] In allusion to the gymnastic training which was *de rigueur* at Sparta for the women no less than the men, and in particular to the dance of the Lacedaemonian girls, in which the performer was expected to kick the fundament with the heels—always a standing joke among the Athenians against their rivals and enemies the Spartans.

[10] The allusion, of course, is to the 'garden of love,' the female parts, which it was the custom with the Greek women, as it is with the ladies of the harem in Turkey to this day, to depilate scrupulously, with the idea of making themselves more attractive to men.

[11] Corinth was notorious in the Ancient world for its prostitutes and general dissoluteness.

LYSISTRATA. I have.

LAMPITO. Well then, tell us what you want of us.

LYSISTRATA. With pleasure, my dear.

MYRRHINÉ. What is the most important business you wish to inform us about?

LYSISTRATA. I will tell you. But first answer me one question.

MYRRHINÉ. What is that?

LYSISTRATA. Don't you feel sad and sorry because the fathers of your children are far away from you with the army? For I'll undertake, there is not one of you whose husband is not abroad at this moment.

CALONICÉ. Mine has been the last five months in Thrace—looking after Eucrates.[12]

LYSISTRATA. 'Tis seven long months since mine left me for Pylos.[13]

LAMPITO. As for mine, if he ever does return from service, he's no sooner back than he takes down his shield again and flies back to the wars.

LYSISTRATA. And not so much as the shadow of a lover! Since the day the Milesians betrayed us, I have never once seen an eight-inch-long *godemiche* even, to be a leathern consolation to us poor widows.... Now tell me, if I have discovered a means of ending the war, will you all second me?

MYRRHINÉ. Yes verily, by all the goddesses, I swear I will, though I have to put my gown in pawn, and drink the money the same day.[14]

CALONICÉ. And so will I, though I must be split in two like a flat-fish, and have half myself removed.

LAMPITO. And I too; why, to secure Peace, I would climb to the top of Mount Taygetus.[15]

LYSISTRATA. Then I will out with it at last, my mighty secret! Oh! sister women, if we would compel our husbands to make peace, we must refrain....

MYRRHINÉ. Refrain from what? tell us, tell us!

LYSISTRATA. But will you do it?

MYRRHINÉ. We will, we will, though we should die of it.

---

[12] An Athenian general strongly suspected of treachery; Aristophanes pretends his own soldiers have to see that he does not desert to the enemy.

[13] A town and fortress on the west coast of Messenia, south-east part of Peloponnese, at the northern extremity of the bay of Sphacteria—the scene by the by of the modern naval battle of Navarino—in Lacedaemonian territory; it had been seized by the Athenian fleet, and was still in their possession at the date, 412 B.C., of the representation of the 'Lysistrata,' though two years later, in the twenty-second year of the War, it was recovered by Sparta.

[14] The Athenian women, rightly or wrongly, had the reputation of being over fond of wine. Aristophanes, here and elsewhere, makes many jests on this weakness of theirs.

[15] The lofty range of hills overlooking Sparta from the west.

LYSISTRATA. We must refrain from the male organ altogether.... Nay, why do you turn your backs on me? Where are you going? So, you bite your lips, and shake your heads, eh? Why these pale, sad looks? why these tears? Come, will you do it—yes or no? Do you hesitate?

MYRRHINÉ. No, I will not do it; let the War go on.

LYSISTRATA. And you, my pretty flat-fish, who declared just now they might split you in two?

CALONICÉ. Anything, anything but that! Bid me go through the fire, if you will; but to rob us of the sweetest thing in all the world, my dear, dear Lysistrata!

LYSISTRATA. And you?

MYRRHINÉ. Yes, I agree with the others; I too would sooner go through the fire.

LYSISTRATA. Oh, wanton, vicious sex! the poets have done well to make tragedies upon us; we are good for nothing then but love and lewdness![16] But you, my dear, you from hardy Sparta, if *you* join me, all may yet be well; help me, second me, I conjure you.

LAMPITO. 'Tis a hard thing, by the two goddesses[17] it is! for a woman to sleep alone without ever a standing weapon in her bed. But there, Peace must come first.

LYSISTRATA. Oh, my dear, my dearest, best friend, you are the only one deserving the name of woman!

CALONICÉ. But if—which the gods forbid—we do refrain altogether from what you say, should we get peace any sooner?

LYSISTRATA. Of course we should, by the goddesses twain! We need only sit indoors with painted cheeks, and meet our mates lightly clad in transparent gowns of Amorgos[18] silk, and with our "mottes" nicely plucked smooth; then their tools will stand like mad and they will be wild to lie with us. That will be the time to refuse, and they will hasten to make peace, I am convinced of that!

LAMPITO. Yes, just as Menelaus, when he saw Helen's naked bosom, threw away his sword, they say.

CALONICÉ. But, poor devils, suppose our husbands go away and leave us.

---

[16] In the original "we are nothing but Poseidon and a boat"; the allusion is to a play of Sophocles, now lost, but familiar to Aristophanes' audience, entitled 'Tyro,' in which the heroine, Tyro, appears with Poseidon, the sea-god, at the beginning of the tragedy, and at the close with the two boys she had had by him, whom she exposes in an open boat.

[17] "By the two goddesses,"—a woman's oath, which recurs constantly in this play; the two goddesses are always Demeter and Proserpine.

[18] One of the Cyclades, between Naxos and Cos, celebrated, like the latter, for its manufacture of fine, almost transparent silks, worn in Greece, and later at Rome, by women of loose character.

LYSISTRATA. Then, as Pherecrates says, we must "flay a skinned dog,"[19] that's all.

CALONICÉ. Bah! these proverbs are all idle talk.... But if our husbands drag us by main force into the bedchamber?

LYSISTRATA. Hold on to the door posts.

CALONICÉ. But if they beat us?

LYSISTRATA. Then yield to their wishes, but with a bad grace; there is no pleasure for them, when they do it by force. Besides, there are a thousand ways of tormenting them. Never fear, they'll soon tire of the game; there's no satisfaction for a man, unless the woman shares it.

CALONICÉ. Very well, if you *will* have it so, we agree.

LAMPITO. For ourselves, no doubt we shall persuade our husbands to conclude a fair and honest peace; but there is the ATHENIAN populace, how are we to cure these folk of their warlike frenzy?

LYSISTRATA. Have no fear; we undertake to make our own people hear reason.

LAMPITO. Nay, impossible, so long as they have their trusty ships and the vast treasures stored in the temple of Athené.

LYSISTRATA. Ah! but we have seen to that; this very day the Acropolis will be in our hands. That is the task assigned to the older women; while we are here in council, they are going, under pretence of offering sacrifice, to seize the citadel.

LAMPITO. Well said indeed! so everything is going for the best.

LYSISTRATA. Come, quick, Lampito, and let us bind ourselves by an inviolable oath.

LAMPITO. Recite the terms; we will swear to them.

LYSISTRATA. With pleasure. Where is our Usheress?[20] Now, what are you staring at, pray? Lay this shield on the earth before us, its hollow upwards, and someone bring me the victim's inwards.

CALONICÉ. Lysistrata, say, what oath are we to swear?

LYSISTRATA. What oath? Why, in Aeschylus, they sacrifice a sheep, and swear over a buckler;[21] we will do the same.

CALONICÉ. No, Lysistrata, one cannot swear peace over a buckler, surely.

LYSISTRATA. What other oath do you prefer?

---

[19] The proverb, quoted by Pherecrates, is properly spoken of those who go out of their way to do a thing already done—"to kill a dead horse," but here apparently is twisted by Aristophanes into an allusion to the leathern 'godemiche' mentioned a little above; if the worst comes to the worst, we must use artificial means. Pherecrates was a comic playwright, a contemporary of Aristophanes.

[20] Literally "our Scythian woman." At Athens, policemen and ushers in the courts were generally Scythians; so the revolting women must have *their* Scythian "Usheress" too.

[21] In allusion to the oath which the seven allied champions before Thebes take upon a buckler, in Aeschylus' tragedy of 'The Seven against Thebes,' v. 42.

CALONICÉ. Let's take a white horse, and sacrifice it, and swear on its entrails.

LYSISTRATA. But where get a white horse from?

CALONICÉ. Well, what oath shall we take then?

LYSISTRATA. Listen to me. Let's set a great black bowl on the ground; let's sacrifice a skin of Thasian[22] wine into it, and take oath not to add one single drop of water.

LAMPITO. Ah! that's an oath pleases me more than I can say.

LYSISTRATA. Let them bring me a bowl and a skin of wine.

CALONICÉ. Ah! my dears, what a noble big bowl! what a delight 'twill be to empty it!

LYSISTRATA. Set the bowl down on the ground, and lay your hands on the victim.... Almighty goddess, Persuasion, and thou, bowl, boon comrade of joy and merriment, receive this our sacrifice, and be propitious to us poor women!

CALONICÉ. Oh! the fine red blood! how well it flows!

LAMPITO. And what a delicious savour, by the goddesses twain!

LYSISTRATA. Now, my dears, let me swear first, if you please.

CALONICÉ. No, by the goddess of love, let us decide that by lot.

LYSISTRATA. Come then, Lampito, and all of you, put your hands to the bowl; and do you, Calonicé, repeat in the name of all the solemn terms I am going to recite. Then you must all swear, and pledge yourselves by the same promises.—"*I will have naught to do whether with lover or husband....*"

CALONICÉ. *I will have naught to do whether with lover or husband....*

LYSISTRATA. *Albeit he come to me with stiff and standing tool....*

CALONICÉ. *Albeit he come to me with stiff and standing tool....* Oh! Lysistrata, I cannot bear it!

LYSISTRATA. *I will live at home in perfect chastity....*

CALONICÉ. *I will live at home in perfect chastity....*

LYSISTRATA. *Beautifully dressed and wearing a saffron-coloured gown....*

CALONICÉ. *Beautifully dressed and wearing a saffron-coloured gown....*

LYSISTRATA. *To the end I may inspire my husband with the most ardent longings.*

CALONICÉ. *To the end I may inspire my husband with the most ardent longings.*

LYSISTRATA. *Never will I give myself voluntarily....*

CALONICÉ. *Never will I give myself voluntarily....*

LYSISTRATA. *And if he has me by force....*

CALONICÉ. *And if he has me by force....*

LYSISTRATA. *I will be cold as ice, and never stir a limb....*

CALONICÉ. *I will be cold as ice, and never stir a limb....*

---

[22] A volcanic island in the northern part of the Aegaean, celebrated for its vineyards.

LYSISTRATA. *I will not lift my legs in air....*

CALONICÉ. *I will not lift my legs in air....*

LYSISTRATA. *Nor will I crouch with bottom upraised, like carven lions on a knife-handle.*

CALONICÉ. *Nor will I crouch with bottom upraised, like carven lions on a knife-handle.*

LYSISTRATA. *And if I keep my oath, may I be suffered to drink of this wine.*

CALONICÉ. *And if I keep my oath, may I be suffered to drink of this wine.*

LYSISTRATA. *But if I break it, let my bowl be filled with water.*

CALONICÉ. *But if I break it, let my bowl be filled with water.*

LYSISTRATA. Will ye all take this oath?

MYRRHINÉ. Yes, yes!

LYSISTRATA. Then lo! I immolate the victim. [*She drinks.*]

CALONICÉ. Enough, enough, my dear; now let us all drink in turn to cement our friendship.

LAMPITO. Hark! what do those cries mean?

LYSISTRATA. 'Tis what I was telling you; the women have just occupied the Acropolis. So now, Lampito, do you return to Sparta to organize the plot, while your comrades here remain as hostages. For ourselves, let us away to join the rest in the citadel, and let us push the bolts well home.

CALONICÉ. But don't you think the men will march up against us?

LYSISTRATA. I laugh at them. Neither threats nor flames shall force our doors; they shall open only on the conditions I have named.

CALONICÉ. Yes, yes, by the goddess of love! let us keep up our old-time repute for obstinacy and spite.

CHORUS OF OLD MEN.[23] Go easy, Draces, go easy; why, your shoulder is all chafed by these plaguey heavy olive stocks. But forward still, forward, man, as needs must. What unlooked-for things do happen, to be sure, in a long life! Ah! Strymodorus, who would ever have thought it? Here we have the women, who used, for our misfortune, to eat our bread and live in our houses, daring nowadays to lay hands on the holy image of the goddess, to seize the Acropolis and draw bars and bolts to keep any from entering! Come, Philurgus man, let's hurry thither; let's lay our faggots all about the citadel, and on the blazing pile burn with our hands these vile conspiratresses, one and all—and Lycon's wife, Lysistrata, first and foremost! Nay, by Demeter, never will I let 'em laugh at

---

[23] The old men are carrying faggots and fire to burn down the gates of the Acropolis, and supply comic material by their panting and wheezing as they climb the steep approaches to the fortress and puff and blow at their fires. Aristophanes gives them names, purely fancy ones—Draces, Strymodorus, Philurgus, Laches.

me, whiles I have a breath left in my body. Cleomenes himself,[24] the first who ever seized our citadel, had to quit it to his sore dishonour; spite his Lacedaemonian pride, he had to deliver me up his arms and slink off with a single garment to his back. My word! but he was filthy and ragged! and what an unkempt beard, to be sure! He had not had a bath for six long years! Oh! but that was a mighty siege! Our men were ranged seventeen deep before the gate, and never left their posts, even to sleep. These women, these enemies of Euripides and all the gods, shall I do nothing to hinder their inordinate insolence? else let them tear down my trophies of Marathon. But look ye, to finish our toilsome climb, we have only this last steep bit left to mount. Verily 'tis no easy job without beasts of burden, and how these logs do bruise my shoulder! Still let us on, and blow up our fire and see it does not go out just as we reach our destination. Phew! phew! [*blows the fire.*] Oh! dear! what a dreadful smoke! it bites my eyes like a mad dog. It is Lemnos[25] fire for sure, or it would never devour my eyelids like this. Come on, Laches, let's hurry, let's bring succour to the goddess; it's now or never! Phew! phew! [*blows the fire.*] Oh! dear! what a confounded smoke!—There now, there's our fire all bright and burning, thank the gods! Now, why not first put down our loads here, then take a vine-branch, light it at the brazier and hurl it at the gate by way of battering-ram? If they don't answer our summons by pulling back the bolts, then we set fire to the woodwork, and the smoke will choke 'em. Ye gods! what a smoke! Pfaugh! Is there never a Samos general will help me unload my burden?[26]—Ah! it shall not gall my shoulder any more. [*Tosses down his wood.*] Come, brazier, do your duty, make the embers flare, that I may kindle a brand; I want to be the first to hurl one. Aid me, heavenly Victory; let us punish for their insolent audacity the women who have seized our citadel, and may we raise a trophy of triumph for success!

CHORUS OF WOMEN.[27] Oh! my dears, methinks I see fire and smoke; can it be a conflagration? Let us hurry all we can. Fly, fly,

---

[24] Cleomenes, King of Sparta, had in the preceding century commanded a Lacedaemonian expedition against Athens. At the invitation of the Alcmaeonidae, enemies of the sons of Peisistratus, he seized the Acropolis, but after an obstinately contested siege was forced to capitulate and retire.

[25] Lemnos was proverbial with the Greeks for chronic misfortune and a succession of horrors and disasters. Can any good thing come out of *Lemnos*?

[26] That is, a friend of the ATHENIAN people; Samos had just before the date of the play re-established the democracy and renewed the old alliance with Athens.

[27] A second Chorus enters—of women who are hurrying up with water to extinguish the fire just started by the Chorus of old men. Nicodicé, Calycé, Crityllé, Rhodippé, are fancy names the poet gives to different members of the band. Another, Stratyllis, has been stopped by the old men on her way to rejoin her companions.

Nicodicé, ere Calycé and Crityllé perish in the fire, or are stifled in the smoke raised by these accursed old men and their pitiless laws. But, great gods, can it be I come too late? Rising at dawn, I had the utmost trouble to fill this vessel at the fountain. Oh! what a crowd there was, and what a din! What a rattling of water-pots! Servants and slave-girls pushed and thronged me! However, here I have it full at last; and I am running to carry the water to my fellow townswomen, whom our foes are plotting to burn alive. News has been brought us that a company of old, doddering greybeards, loaded with enormous faggots, as if they wanted to heat a furnace, have taken the field, vomiting dreadful threats, crying that they must reduce to ashes these horrible women. Suffer them not, oh! goddess, but, of thy grace, may I see Athens and Greece cured of their warlike folly. 'Tis to this end, oh! thou guardian deity of our city, goddess of the golden crest, that they have seized thy sanctuary. Be their friend and ally, Athené, and if any man hurl against them lighted firebrands, aid us to carry water to extinguish them.

STRATYLLIS. Let me be, I say. Oh! oh! [*She calls for help.*]

CHORUS OF WOMEN. What is this I see, ye wretched old men? Honest and pious folk ye cannot be who act so vilely.

CHORUS OF OLD MEN. Ah, ha! here's something new! a swarm of women stand posted outside to defend the gates!

CHORUS OF WOMEN. Ah! ah! we frighten you, do we; we seem a mighty host, yet you do not see the ten-thousandth part of our sex.

CHORUS OF OLD MEN. Ho, Phaedrias! shall we stop their cackle? Suppose one of us were to break a stick across their backs, eh?

CHORUS OF WOMEN. Let us set down our water-pots on the ground, to be out of the way, if they should dare to offer us violence.

CHORUS OF OLD MEN. Let someone knock out two or three teeth for them, as they did to Bupalus;[28] they won't talk so loud then.

CHORUS OF WOMEN. Come on then; I wait you with unflinching foot, and I will snap off your testicles like a bitch.

CHORUS OF OLD MEN. Silence! ere my stick has cut short your days.

CHORUS OF WOMEN. Now, just you dare to touch Stratyllis with the tip of your finger!

CHORUS OF OLD MEN. And if I batter you to pieces with my fists, what will you do?

CHORUS OF WOMEN. I will tear out your lungs and entrails with my teeth.

---

[28] Bupalus was a celebrated contemporary sculptor, a native of Clazomenae. The satiric poet Hipponax, who was extremely ugly, having been portrayed by Bupalus as even more unsightly-looking than the reality, composed against the artist so scurrilous an invective that the latter hung himself in despair. Apparently Aristophanes alludes here to a verse in which Hipponax threatened to beat Bupalus.

CHORUS OF OLD MEN. Oh! what a clever poet is Euripides! how well he says that woman is the most shameless of animals.

CHORUS OF WOMEN. Let's pick up our water-jars again, Rhodippé.

CHORUS OF OLD MEN. Ah! accursed harlot, what do you mean to do here with your water?

CHORUS OF WOMEN. And you, old death-in-life, with your fire? Is it to cremate yourself?

CHORUS OF OLD MEN. I am going to build you a pyre to roast your female friends upon.

CHORUS OF WOMEN. And I,—I am going to put out your fire.

CHORUS OF OLD MEN. You put out my fire—you!

CHORUS OF WOMEN. Yes, you shall soon see.

CHORUS OF OLD MEN. I don't know what prevents me from roasting you with this torch.

CHORUS OF WOMEN. I am getting you a bath ready to clean off the filth.

CHORUS OF OLD MEN. A bath for me, you dirty slut, you!

CHORUS OF WOMEN. Yes, indeed, a nuptial bath—he, he!

CHORUS OF OLD MEN. Do you hear that? What insolence!

CHORUS OF WOMEN. I am a free woman, I tell you.

CHORUS OF OLD MEN. I will make you hold your tongue, never fear!

CHORUS OF WOMEN. Ah, ha! you shall never sit more amongst the Heliasts.[29]

CHORUS OF OLD MEN. Burn off her hair for her!

CHORUS OF WOMEN. Water, do your office! [*The women pitch the water in their water-pots over the old men.*]

CHORUS OF OLD MEN. Oh, dear! oh, dear! oh, dear!

CHORUS OF WOMEN. Was it hot?

CHORUS OF OLD MEN. Hot, great gods! Enough, enough!

CHORUS OF WOMEN. I'm watering you, to make you bloom afresh.

CHORUS OF OLD MEN. Alas! I am too dry! Ah, me! how I am trembling with cold!

MAGISTRATE. These women, have they made din enough, I wonder, with their tambourines? bewept Adonis enough upon their terraces?[30] I was listening to the speeches last assembly day,[31] and

---

[29] The Heliasts at Athens were the body of citizens chosen by lot to act as jurymen (or, more strictly speaking, as judges and jurymen, the Dicast, or so-called Judge, being merely President of the Court, the majority of the Heliasts pronouncing sentence) in the Heliaia, or High Court, where all offences liable to public prosecution were tried. They were 6000 in number, divided into ten panels of 500 each, a thousand being held in reserve to supply occasional vacancies. Each Heliast was paid three obols for each day's attendance in court.

[30] Women only celebrated the festivals of Adonis. These rites were not performed in public, but on the terraces and flat roofs of the houses.

Demostratus,[32] whom heaven confound! was saying we must all go over to Sicily—and lo! his wife was dancing round repeating: Alas! alas! Adonis, woe is me for Adonis!

Demostratus was saying we must levy hoplites at Zacynthus[33]—and lo! his wife, more than half drunk, was screaming on the house-roof: "Weep, weep for Adonis!"—while that infamous *Mad Ox*[34] was bellowing away on his side.—Do ye not blush, ye women, for your wild and uproarious doings?

CHORUS OF OLD MEN. But you don't know all their effrontery yet! They abused and insulted us; then soused us with the water in their water-pots, and have set us wringing out our clothes, for all the world as if we had bepissed ourselves.

MAGISTRATE. And 'tis well done too, by Poseidon! We men must share the blame of their ill conduct; it is we who teach them to love riot and dissoluteness and sow the seeds of wickedness in their hearts. You see a husband go into a shop: "Look you, jeweller," says he, "you remember the necklace you made for my wife. Well, t'other evening, when she was dancing, the catch came open. Now, I am bound to start for Salamis; will you make it convenient to go up to-night to make her fastening secure?" Another will go to a cobbler, a great, strong fellow, with a great, long tool, and tell him: "The strap of one of my wife's sandals presses her little toe, which is extremely sensitive; come in about midday to supple the thing and stretch it." Now see the results. Take my own case—as a Magistrate I have enlisted rowers; I want money to pay 'em, and lo! the women clap to the door in my face.[35] But why do we stand here with arms crossed? Bring me a crowbar; I'll chastise their insolence!—Ho! there, my fine fellow! [*addressing one of his attendant officers*] what are you gaping at the crows about? looking for a tavern, I suppose, eh? Come, crowbars here, and force open the gates. I will put a hand to the work myself.

LYSISTRATA. No need to force the gates; I am coming out—here I am. And why bolts and bars? What we want here is not bolts and bars and locks, but common sense.

MAGISTRATE. Really, my fine lady! Where is my officer? I want him to tie that woman's hands behind her back.

---

[31] The Assembly, or Ecclesia, was the General Parliament of the ATHENIAN people, in which every adult citizen had a vote. It met on the Pnyx hill, where the assembled Ecclesiasts were addressed from the Bema, or speaking-block.

[32] An orator and statesman who had first proposed the disastrous Sicilian Expedition, of 415-413 B.C. This was on the first day of the festival of Adonis—ever afterwards regarded by the Athenians as a day of ill omen.

[33] An island in the Ionian Sea, on the west of Greece, near Cephalenia, and an ally of Athens during the Peloponnesian War.

[34] Cholozyges, a nickname for Demostratus.

[35] The State treasure was kept in the Acropolis, which the women had seized.

LYSISTRATA. By Artemis, the virgin goddess! if he touches me with the tip of his finger, officer of the public peace though he be, let him look out for himself!

MAGISTRATE. [*to the officer.*] How now, are you afraid? Seize her, I tell you, round the body. Two of you at her, and have done with it!

FIRST WOMAN. By Pandrosos! if you lay a hand on her, I'll trample you underfoot till you shit your guts!

MAGISTRATE. Oh, there! my guts! Where is my other officer? Bind that minx first, who speaks so prettily!

SECOND WOMAN. By Phoebé, if you touch her with one finger, you'd better call quick for a surgeon!

MAGISTRATE. What do you mean? Officer, where are you got to? Lay hold of her. Oh! but I'm going to stop your foolishness for you all!

THIRD WOMAN. By the Tauric Artemis, if you go near her, I'll pull out your hair, scream as you like.

MAGISTRATE. Ah! miserable man that I am! My own officers desert me. What ho! are we to let ourselves be bested by a mob of women? Ho! Scythians mine, close up your ranks, and forward!

LYSISTRATA. By the holy goddesses! you'll have to make acquaintance with four companies of women, ready for the fray and well armed to boot.

MAGISTRATE. Forward, Scythians, and bind them!

LYSISTRATA. Forward, my gallant companions; march forth, ye vendors of grain and eggs, garlic and vegetables, keepers of taverns and bakeries, wrench and strike and tear; come, a torrent of invective and insult! [*They beat the officers.*] Enough, enough! now retire, never rob the vanquished!

MAGISTRATE. Here's a fine exploit for my officers!

LYSISTRATA. Ah, ha! so you thought you had only to do with a set of slave-women! you did not know the ardour that fills the bosom of free-born dames.

MAGISTRATE. Ardour! yes, by Apollo, ardour enough—especially for the wine-cup!

CHORUS OF OLD MEN. Sir, sir! what use of words? they are of no avail with wild beasts of this sort. Don't you know how they have just washed us down—and with no very fragrant soap!

CHORUS OF WOMEN. What would you have? You should never have laid rash hands on us. If you start afresh, I'll knock your eyes out. My delight is to stay at home as coy as a young maid, without hurting anybody or moving any more than a milestone; but 'ware the wasps, if you go stirring up the wasps' nest!

CHORUS OF OLD MEN. Ah! great gods! how get the better of these ferocious creatures? 'tis past all bearing! But come, let us try to find out the reason of the dreadful scourge. With what end in view have they seized the citadel of Cranaus,[36] the sacred shrine that is raised upon the inaccessible rock of the Acropolis? Question them; be cautious and not too credulous. 'Twould be culpable negligence not to pierce the mystery, if we may.

MAGISTRATE. [*addressing the women.*] I would ask you first why ye have barred our gates.

LYSISTRATA. To seize the treasury; no more money, no more war.

MAGISTRATE. Then money is the cause of the War?

LYSISTRATA. And of all our troubles. 'Twas to find occasion to steal that Pisander[37] and all the other agitators were for ever raising revolutions. Well and good! but they'll never get another drachma here.

MAGISTRATE. What do you propose to do then, pray?

LYSISTRATA. You ask me that! Why, we propose to administer the treasury ourselves.

MAGISTRATE. *You* do?

LYSISTRATA. What is there in that to surprise you? Do we not administer the budget of household expenses?

MAGISTRATE. But that is not the same thing.

LYSISTRATA How so—not the same thing?

MAGISTRATE. It is the treasury supplies the expenses of the War.

LYSISTRATA. That's our first principle—no War!

MAGISTRATE. What! and the safety of the city?

LYSISTRATA. We will provide for that.

MAGISTRATE You?

LYSISTRATA Yes, just we.

MAGISTRATE. What a sorry business!

LYSISTRATA. Yes, we're going to save you, whether you will or no.

MAGISTRATE. Oh! the impudence of the creatures!

LYSISTRATA. You seem annoyed! but there, you've got to come to it.

MAGISTRATE. But 'tis the very height of iniquity!

LYSISTRATA. We're going to save you, my man.

MAGISTRATE. But if I don't want to be saved?

LYSISTRATA. Why, all the more reason!

MAGISTRATE. But what a notion, to concern yourselves with questions of Peace and War!

LYSISTRATA. We will explain our idea.

MAGISTRATE. Out with it then; quick, or … [*threatening her.*]

LYSISTRATA. Listen, and never a movement, please!

MAGISTRATE. Oh! it is too much for me! I cannot keep my temper!

---

[36] The second (mythical) king of Athens, successor of Cecrops.

[37] The leader of the Revolution which resulted in the temporary overthrow of the Democracy at Athens (413, 412 B.C.), and the establishment of the Oligarchy of the Four Hundred.

A WOMAN. Then look out for yourself; you have more to fear than we have.

MAGISTRATE. Stop your croaking, old crow, you! [*To Lysistrata.*] Now you, say your say.

LYSISTRATA. Willingly. All the long time the War has lasted, we have endured in modest silence all you men did; we never allowed ourselves to open our lips. We were far from satisfied, for we knew how things were going; often in our homes we would hear you discussing, upside down and inside out, some important turn of affairs. Then with sad hearts, but smiling lips, we would ask you: Well, in to-day's Assembly did they vote Peace?—But, "Mind your own business!" the husband would growl, "Hold your tongue, do!" And I would say no more.

A WOMAN. I would not have held my tongue though, not I!

MAGISTRATE. You would have been reduced to silence by blows then.

LYSISTRATA. Well, for my part, I would say no more. But presently I would come to know you had arrived at some fresh decision more fatally foolish than ever. "Ah! my dear man," I would say, "what madness next!" But he would only look at me askance and say: "Just weave your web, do; else your cheeks will smart for hours. War is men's business!"

MAGISTRATE. Bravo! well said indeed!

LYSISTRATA. How now, wretched man? not to let us contend against your follies, was bad enough! But presently we heard you asking out loud in the open street: "Is there never a man left in Athens?" and, "No, not one, not one," you were assured in reply. Then, then we made up our minds without more delay to make common cause to save Greece. Open your ears to our wise counsels and hold your tongues, and we may yet put things on a better footing.

MAGISTRATE. *You* put things indeed! Oh! 'tis too much! The insolence of the creatures! Silence, I say.

LYSISTRATA. Silence yourself!

MAGISTRATE. May I die a thousand deaths ere I obey one who wears a veil!

LYSISTRATA. If that's all that troubles you, here, take my veil, wrap it round your head, and hold your tongue. Then take this basket; put on a girdle, card wool, munch beans. The War shall be women's business.

CHORUS OF WOMEN. Lay aside your water-pots, we will guard them, we will help our friends and companions. For myself, I will never weary of the dance; my knees will never grow stiff with fatigue. I will brave everything with my dear allies, on whom Nature has lavished virtue, grace, boldness, cleverness, and whose wisely directed energy is going to save the State. Oh! my good, gallant

Lysistrata, and all my friends, be ever like a bundle of nettles; never let your anger slacken; the winds of fortune blow our way.

LYSISTRATA. May gentle Love and the sweet Cyprian Queen shower seductive charms on our bosoms and all our person. If only we may stir so amorous a lust among the men that their tools stand stiff as sticks, we shall indeed deserve the name of peace-makers among the Greeks.

MAGISTRATE. How will that be, pray?

LYSISTRATA. To begin with, we shall not see you any more running like mad fellows to the Market holding lance in fist.

A WOMAN. That will be something gained, anyway, by the Paphian goddess, it will!

LYSISTRATA. Now we see 'em, mixed up with saucepans and kitchen stuff, armed to the teeth, looking like wild Corybantes![38]

MAGISTRATE. Why, of course; that's how brave men should do.

LYSISTRATA. Oh! but what a funny sight, to behold a man wearing a Gorgon's-head buckler coming along to buy fish!

A WOMAN. 'Tother day in the Market I saw a phylarch[39] with flowing ringlets; he was a-horseback, and was pouring into his helmet the broth he had just bought at an old dame's stall. There was a Thracian warrior too, who was brandishing his lance like Tereus in the play;[40] he had scared a good woman selling figs into a perfect panic, and was gobbling up all her ripest fruit.

MAGISTRATE. And how, pray, would you propose to restore peace and order in all the countries of Greece?

LYSISTRATA. 'Tis the easiest thing in the world!

MAGISTRATE. Come, tell us how; I am curious to know.

LYSISTRATA. When we are winding thread, and it is tangled, we pass the spool across and through the skein, now this way, now that way; even so, to finish off the War, we shall send embassies hither and thither and everywhere, to disentangle matters.

MAGISTRATE. And 'tis with your yarn, and your skeins, and your spools, you think to appease so many bitter enmities, you silly women?

LYSISTRATA. If only you had common sense, you would always do in politics the same as we do with our yarn.

MAGISTRATE. Come, how is that, eh?

LYSISTRATA. First we wash the yarn to separate the grease and filth; do the same with all bad citizens, sort them out and drive them forth

---

[38] Priests of Cybelé, who indulged in wild, frenzied dances, to the accompaniment of the clashing of cymbals, in their celebrations in honour of the goddess.

[39] Captain of a cavalry division; they were chosen from amongst the *Hippeis*, or 'Knights' at Athens.

[40] In allusion to a play of Euripides, now lost, with this title. Tereus was son of Ares and king of the Thracians in Daulis.

with rods—'tis the refuse of the city. Then for all such as come crowding up in search of employments and offices, we must card them thoroughly; then, to bring them all to the same standard, pitch them pell-mell into the same basket, resident aliens or no, allies, debtors to the State, all mixed up together. Then as for our Colonies, you must think of them as so many isolated hanks; find the ends of the separate threads, draw them to a centre here, wind them into one, make one great hank of the lot, out of which the Public can weave itself a good, stout tunic.

MAGISTRATE. Is it not a sin and a shame to see them carding and winding the State, these women who have neither art nor part in the burdens of the War?

LYSISTRATA. What! wretched man! why, 'tis a far heavier burden to us than to you. In the first place, we bear sons who go off to fight far away from Athens.

MAGISTRATE. Enough said! do not recall sad and sorry memories![41]

LYSISTRATA. Then secondly, instead of enjoying the pleasures of love and making the best of our youth and beauty, we are left to languish far from our husbands, who are all with the army. But say no more of ourselves; what afflicts me is to see our girls growing old in lonely grief.

MAGISTRATE. Don't the men grow old too?

LYSISTRATA. That is not the same thing. When the soldier returns from the wars, even though he has white hair, he very soon finds a young wife. But a woman has only one summer; if she does not make hay while the sun shines, no one will afterwards have anything to say to her, and she spends her days consulting oracles, that never send her a husband.

MAGISTRATE. But the old man who can still erect his organ ...

LYSISTRATA. But you, why don't you get done with it and die? You are rich; go buy yourself a bier, and I will knead you a honey-cake for Cerberus. Here, take this garland. [*Drenching him with water.*]

FIRST WOMAN. And this one too. [*Drenching him with water.*]

SECOND WOMAN. And these fillets. [*Drenching him with water.*]

LYSISTRATA. What do you lack more? Step aboard the boat; Charon is waiting for you, you're keeping him from pushing off.

MAGISTRATE. To treat me so scurvily! What an insult! I will go show myself to my fellow-magistrates just as I am.

LYSISTRATA. What! are you blaming us for not having exposed you according to custom?[42] Nay, console yourself; we will not fail to offer up the third-day sacrifice for you, first thing in the morning.[43]

---

[41] An allusion to the disastrous Sicilian Expedition (415-413 B.C.), in which many thousands of ATHENIAN citizens perished.

[42] The dead were laid out at Athens before the house door.

[43] An offering made to the Manes of the deceased on the third day after the funeral.

CHORUS OF OLD MEN. Awake, friends of freedom; let us hold ourselves aye ready to act. I suspect a mighty peril; I foresee another Tyranny like Hippias'.[44] I am sore afraid the Laconians assembled here with Cleisthenes have, by a stratagem of war, stirred up these women, enemies of the gods, to seize upon our treasury and the funds whereby I lived.[45] Is it not a sin and a shame for them to interfere in advising the citizens, to prate of shields and lances, and to ally themselves with Laconians, fellows I trust no more than I would so many famished wolves? The whole thing, my friends, is nothing else but an attempt to re-establish Tyranny. But I will never submit; I will be on my guard for the future; I will always carry a blade hidden under myrtle boughs; I will post myself in the Public Square under arms, shoulder to shoulder with Aristogiton;[46] and now, to make a start, I must just break a few of that cursed old jade's teeth yonder.

CHORUS OF WOMEN. Nay, never play the brave man, else when you go back home, your own mother won't know you. But, dear friends and allies, first let us lay our burdens down; then, citizens all, hear what I have to say. I have useful counsel to give our city, which deserves it well at my hands for the brilliant distinctions it has lavished on my girlhood. At seven years of age, I was bearer of the sacred vessels; at ten, I pounded barley for the altar of Athené; next, clad in a robe of yellow silk, I was *little bear* to Artemis at the Brauronia;[47] presently, grown a tall, handsome maiden, they put a necklace of dried figs about my neck, and I was Basket-Bearer.[48] So surely I am bound to give my best advice to Athens. What matters that I was born a woman, if I can cure your misfortunes? I pay my share of tolls and taxes, by giving men to the State. But you, you miserable greybeards, you contribute

---

[44] Hippias and Hipparchus, the two sons of Pisistratus, known as the Pisistratidae, became Tyrants of Athens upon their father's death in 527 B.C. In 514 the latter was assassinated by the conspirators, Harmodius and Aristogiton, who took the opportunity of the Panathenaic festival and concealed their daggers in myrtle wreaths. They were put to death, but four years later the surviving Tyrant Hippias was expelled, and the young and noble martyrs to liberty were ever after held in the highest honour by their fellow-citizens. Their statues stood in the Agora or Public Market-Square.

[45] That is, the three obols paid for attendance as a Heliast at the High Court.

[46] See above, under note 44.

[47] The origin of the name was this: in ancient days a tame bear consecrated to Artemis, the huntress goddess, it seems, devoured a young girl, whose brothers killed the offender. Artemis was angered and sent a terrible pestilence upon the city, which only ceased when, by direction of the oracle, a company of maidens was dedicated to the deity, to act the part of she-bears in the festivities held annually in her honour at the Brauronia, her festival so named from the deme of Brauron in Attica.

[48] The Basket-Bearers, Canephoroi, at Athens were the maidens who, clad in flowing robes, carried in baskets on their heads the sacred implements and paraphernalia in procession at the celebrations in honour of Demeter, Dionysus and Athené.

nothing to the public charges; on the contrary, you have wasted the treasure of our forefathers, as it was called, the treasure amassed in the days of the Persian Wars.[49] You pay nothing at all in return; and into the bargain you endanger our lives and liberties by your mistakes. Have you one word to say for yourselves? ... Ah! don't irritate me, you there, or I'll lay my slipper across your jaws; and it's pretty heavy.

CHORUS OF OLD MEN. Outrage upon outrage! things are going from bad to worse. Let us punish the minxes, every one of us that has a man's appendages to boast of. Come, off with our tunics, for a man must savour of manhood; come, my friends, let us strip naked from head to foot. Courage, I say, we who in our day garrisoned Lipsydrion;[50] let us be young again, and shake off eld. If we give them the least hold over us, 'tis all up! their audacity will know no bounds! We shall see them building ships, and fighting sea-fights, like Artemisia;[51] nay, if they want to mount and ride as cavalry, we had best cashier the knights, for indeed women excel in riding, and have a fine, firm seat for the gallop.[52] Just think of all those squadrons of Amazons Micon has painted for us engaged in hand-to-hand combat with men.[53] Come then, we must e'en fit collars to all these willing necks.

CHORUS OF WOMEN. By the blessed goddesses, if you anger me, I will let loose the beast of my evil passions, and a very hailstorm of blows will set you yelling for help. Come, dames, off tunics, and quick's the word; women must scent the savour of women in the throes of passion.... Now just you dare to measure strength with me, old greybeard, and I warrant you you'll never eat garlic or black beans more. No, not a word! my anger is at boiling point, and I'll do with you what the beetle did with the eagle's eggs.[54] I

---

[49] A treasure formed by voluntary contributions at the time of the Persian Wars; by Aristophanes' day it had all been dissipated, through the influence of successive demagogues, in distributions and gifts to the public under various pretexts.

[50] A town and fortress of Southern Attica, in the neighbourhood of Marathon, occupied by the Alcmaeonidae—the noble family or clan at Athens banished from the city in 595 B.C., restored 560, but again expelled by Pisistratus—in the course of their contest with that Tyrant. Returning to Athens on the death of Hippias (510 B.C.), they united with the democracy, and the then head of the family, Cleisthenes, gave a new constitution to the city.

[51] Queen of Halicarnassus, in Caria; an ally of the Persian King Xerxes in his invasion of Greece; she fought gallantly at the battle of Salamis.

[52] A *double entendre*—with allusion to the posture in sexual intercourse known among the Greeks as ἵππος, in Latin 'equus,' the horse, where the woman mounts the man in reversal of the ordinary position.

[53] Micon, a famous ATHENIAN painter, decorated the walls of the Poecilé Stoa, or Painted Porch, at Athens with a series of frescoes representing the battles of the Amazons with Theseus and the Athenians.

[54] To avenge itself on the eagle, the beetle threw the former's eggs out of the nest and broke them. See the Fables of Aesop.

laugh at your threats, so long as I have on my side Lampito here, and the noble Theban, my dear Ismenia.... Pass decree on decree, you can do us no hurt, you wretch abhorred of all your fellows. Why, only yesterday, on occasion of the feast of Hecaté, I asked my neighbours of Boeotia for one of their daughters for whom my girls have a lively liking—a fine, fat eel to wit; and if they did not refuse, all along of your silly decrees! We shall never cease to suffer the like, till someone gives you a neat trip-up and breaks your neck for you!

[*Several days are supposed to have elapsed.*]

CHORUS OF WOMEN. [*addressing Lysistrata.*] You, Lysistrata, you who are leader of our glorious enterprise, why do I see you coming towards me with so gloomy an air?

LYSISTRATA. 'Tis the behaviour of these naughty women, 'tis the female heart and female weakness so discourages me.

CHORUS OF WOMEN. Tell us, tell us, what is it?

LYSISTRATA. I only tell the simple truth.

CHORUS OF WOMEN. What has happened so disconcerting; come, tell your friends.

LYSISTRATA. Oh! the thing is so hard to tell—yet so impossible to conceal.

CHORUS OF WOMEN. Nay, never seek to hide any ill that has befallen our cause.

LYSISTRATA. To blurt it out in a word—we are in heat!

CHORUS OF WOMEN. Oh! Zeus, oh! Zeus!

LYSISTRATA. What use calling upon Zeus? The thing is even as I say. I cannot stop them any longer from lusting after the men. They are all for deserting. The first I caught was slipping out by the postern gate near the cave of Pan; another was letting herself down by a rope and pulley; a third was busy preparing her escape; while a fourth, perched on a bird's back, was just taking wing for Orsilochus' house,[55] when I seized her by the hair. One and all, they are inventing excuses to be off home. Look! there goes one, trying to get out! Halloa there! whither away so fast?

FIRST WOMAN. I want to go home; I have some Miletus wool in the house, which is getting all eaten up by the worms.

LYSISTRATA. Bah! you and your worms! go back, I say!

FIRST WOMAN. I will return immediately, I swear I will by the two goddesses! I only have just to spread it out on the bed.

LYSISTRATA. You shall not do anything of the kind! I say, you shall not go.

---

[55] Keeper of a house of ill fame apparently.

FIRST WOMAN. Must I leave my wool to spoil then?

LYSISTRATA. Yes, if need be.

SECOND WOMAN. Unhappy woman that I am! Alas for my flax! I've left it at home unstript!

LYSISTRATA. So, here's another trying to escape to go home and strip her flax forsooth!

SECOND WOMAN. Oh! I swear by the goddess of light, the instant I have put it in condition I will come straight back.

LYSISTRATA. You shall do nothing of the kind! If once you began, others would want to follow suit.

THIRD WOMAN. Oh! goddess divine, Ilithyia, patroness of women in labour, stay, stay the birth, till I have reached a spot less hallowed than Athené's Mount!

LYSISTRATA. What mean you by these silly tales?

THIRD WOMAN. I am going to have a child—now, this minute.

LYSISTRATA. But you were not pregnant yesterday!

THIRD WOMAN. Well, I am to-day. Oh! let me go in search of the midwife, Lysistrata, quick, quick!

LYSISTRATA. What is this fable you are telling me? Ah! what have you got there so hard?

THIRD WOMAN. A male child.

LYSISTRATA. No, no, by Aphrodité! nothing of the sort! Why, it feels like something hollow—a pot or a kettle. Oh! you baggage, if you have not got the sacred helmet of Pallas—and you said you were with child!

THIRD WOMAN. And so I am, by Zeus, I am!

LYSISTRATA. Then why this helmet, pray?

THIRD WOMAN. For fear my pains should seize me in the Acropolis; I mean to lay my eggs in this helmet, as the doves do.

LYSISTRATA. Excuses and pretences every word! the thing's as clear as daylight. Anyway, you must stay here now till the fifth day, your day of purification.

THIRD WOMAN. I cannot sleep any more in the Acropolis, now I have seen the snake that guards the Temple.

FOURTH WOMAN. Ah! and those confounded owls with their dismal hooting! I cannot get a wink of rest, and I'm just dying of fatigue.

LYSISTRATA. You wicked women, have done with your falsehoods! You want your husbands, that's plain enough. But don't you think they want you just as badly? They are spending dreadful nights, oh! I know that well enough. But hold out, my dears, hold out! A little more patience, and the victory will be ours. An Oracle promises us success, if only we remain united. Shall I repeat the words?

FIRST WOMAN. Yes, tell us what the Oracle declares.

LYSISTRATA. Silence then! Now—"Whenas the swallows, fleeing before the hoopoes, shall have all flocked together in one place, and shall refrain them from all amorous commerce, then will be the end of all the ills of life; yea, and Zeus, which doth thunder in the skies, shall set above what was erst below...."

CHORUS OF WOMEN. What! shall the men be underneath?

LYSISTRATA. "But if dissension do arise among the swallows, and they take wing from the holy Temple, 'twill be said there is never a more wanton bird in all the world."

CHORUS OF WOMEN. Ye gods! the prophecy is clear. Nay, never let us be cast down by calamity! let us be brave to bear, and go back to our posts. 'Twere shameful indeed not to trust the promises of the Oracle.

CHORUS OF OLD MEN. I want to tell you a fable they used to relate to me when I was a little boy. This is it: Once upon a time there was a young man called Melanion, who hated the thought of marriage so sorely that he fled away to the wilds. So he dwelt in the mountains, wove himself nets, kept a dog and caught hares. He never, never came back, he had such a horror of women. As chaste as Melanion,[56] we loathe the jades just as much as he did.

AN OLD MAN. You dear old woman, I would fain kiss you.

A WOMAN. I will set you crying without onions.

OLD MAN. ... And give you a sound kicking.

OLD WOMAN. Ah, ha! what a dense forest you have there! [*Pointing.*]

OLD MAN. So was Myronides one of the best-bearded of men o' this side; his backside was all black, and he terrified his enemies as much as Phormio.[57]

CHORUS OF WOMEN. I want to tell you a fable too, to match yours about Melanion. Once there was a certain man called Timon,[58] a tough customer, and a whimsical, a true son of the Furies, with a face that seemed to glare out of a thorn-bush. He withdrew from the world because he couldn't abide bad men, after vomiting a thousand curses at 'em. He had a holy horror of ill-conditioned fellows, but he was mighty tender towards women.

A WOMAN. Suppose I up and broke your jaw for you!

AN OLD MAN. I am not a bit afraid of you.

A WOMAN. Suppose I let fly a good kick at you?

---

[56] "As chaste as Melanion" was a Greek proverb. Who Melanion was is unknown.

[57] Myronides and Phormio were famous ATHENIAN generals. The former was celebrated for his conquest of all Bocotia, except Thebes, in 458 B.C.; the latter, with a fleet of twenty triremes, equipped at his own cost, defeated a Lacedaemonian fleet of forty-seven sail, in 429.

[58] Timon, the misanthrope; he was an ATHENIAN and a contemporary of Aristophanes. Disgusted by the ingratitude of his fellow-citizens and sickened with repeated disappointments, he retired altogether from society, admitting no one, it is said, to his intimacy except the brilliant young statesman Alcibiades.

OLD MAN. I should see your backside then.
WOMAN. You would see that, for all my age, it is very well attended to, and all fresh singed smooth.
LYSISTRATA. Ho there! come quick, come quick!
FIRST WOMAN. What is it? Why these cries?
LYSISTRATA. A man! a man! I see him approaching all afire with the flames of love. Oh! divine Queen of Cyprus, Paphos and Cythera, I pray you still be propitious to our emprise.
FIRST WOMAN. Where is he, this unknown foe?
LYSISTRATA. Yonder—beside the Temple of Demeter.
FIRST WOMAN. Yes, indeed, I see him; but who is it?
LYSISTRATA. Look, look! does any of you recognize him?
FIRST WOMAN. I do, I do! 'tis my husband Cinesias.
LYSISTRATA. To work then! Be it your task to inflame and torture and torment him. Seductions, caresses, provocations, refusals, try every means! Grant every favour,—always excepting what is forbidden by our oath on the wine-bowl.
MYRRHINÉ. Have no fear, I undertake the work.
LYSISTRATA. Well, I will stay here to help you cajole the man and set his passions aflame. The rest of you, withdraw.
CINESIAS. Alas! alas! how I am tortured by spasm and rigid convulsion! Oh! I am racked on the wheel!
LYSISTRATA. Who is this that dares to pass our lines?
CINESIAS. It is I.
LYSISTRATA. What, a man?
CINESIAS. Yes, no doubt about it, a man!
LYSISTRATA. Begone!
CINESIAS. But who are you that thus repulses me?
LYSISTRATA. The sentinel of the day.
CINESIAS. By all the gods, call Myrrhiné hither.
LYSISTRATA. Call Myrrhiné hither, quotha? And pray, who are you?
CINESIAS. I am her husband, Cinesias, son of Peon.
LYSISTRATA. Ah! good day, my dear friend. Your name is not unknown amongst us. Your wife has it forever on her lips; and she never touches an egg or an apple without saying: "'Twill be for Cinesias."
CINESIAS. Really and truly?
LYSISTRATA. Yes, indeed, by Aphrodité! And if we fall to talking of men, quick your wife declares: "Oh! all the rest, they're good for nothing compared with Cinesias."
CINESIAS. Oh! I beseech you, go and call her to me.
LYSISTRATA. And what will you give me for my trouble?
CINESIAS. This, if you like [*handling his tool.*] I will give you what I have there!
LYSISTRATA. Well, well, I will tell her to come.

CINESIAS. Quick, oh! be quick! Life has no more charms for me since she left my house. I am sad, sad, when I go indoors; it all seems so empty; my victuals have lost their savour. Desire is eating out my heart!

MYRRHINÉ. I love him, oh! I love him; but he won't let himself be loved. No! I shall not come.

CINESIAS. Myrrhiné, my little darling Myrrhiné, what are you saying? Come down to me quick.

MYRRHINÉ. No indeed, not I.

CINESIAS. I call you, Myrrhiné, Myrrhiné; will you not come?

MYRRHINÉ. Why should you call me? You do not want me.

CINESIAS. Not want you! Why, my weapon stands stiff with desire!

MYRRHINÉ. Good-bye.

CINESIAS. Oh! Myrrhiné, Myrrhiné, in our child's name, hear me; at any rate hear the child! Little lad, call your mother.

CHILD. Mammy, mammy, mammy!

CINESIAS. There, listen! Don't you pity the poor child? It's six days now you've never washed and never fed the child.

MYRRHINÉ. Poor darling, your father takes mighty little care of you!

CINESIAS. Come down, dearest, come down for the child's sake.

MYRRHINÉ. Ah! what a thing it is to be a mother! Well, well, we must come down, I suppose.

CINESIAS. Why, how much younger and prettier she looks! And how she looks at me so lovingly! Her cruelty and scorn only redouble my passion.

MYRRHINÉ. You are as sweet as your father is provoking! Let me kiss you, my treasure, mother's darling!

CINESIAS. Ah! what a bad thing it is to let yourself be led away by other women! Why give me such pain and suffering, and yourself into the bargain?

MYRRHINÉ. Hands off, sir!

CINESIAS. Everything is going to rack and ruin in the house.

MYRRHINÉ. I don't care.

CINESIAS. But your web that's all being pecked to pieces by the cocks and hens, don't you care for that?

MYRRHINÉ. Precious little.

CINESIAS. And Aphrodite, whose mysteries you have not celebrated for so long? Oh! won't you come back home?

MYRRHINÉ. No, at least, not till a sound Treaty put an end to the War.

CINESIAS. Well, if you wish it so much, why, we'll make it, your Treaty.

MYRRHINÉ. Well and good! When that's done, I will come home. Till then, I am bound by an oath.

CINESIAS. At any rate, let's have a short time together.

MYRRHINÉ. No, no, no! … all the same I cannot say I don't love you.

CINESIAS. You love me? Then why refuse what I ask, my little girl, my sweet Myrrhiné.

MYRRHINÉ. You must be joking! What, before the child!

CINESIAS. Manes, carry the lad home. There, you see, the child is gone; there's nothing to hinder us; let us to work!

MYRRHINÉ. But, miserable man, where, where are we to do it?

CINESIAS. In the cave of Pan; nothing could be better.

MYRRHINÉ. But how to purify myself, before going back into the citadel?

CINESIAS. Nothing easier! you can wash at the Clepsydra.[59]

MYRRHINÉ. But my oath? Do you want me to perjure myself?

CINESIAS. I take all responsibility; never make yourself anxious.

MYRRHINÉ. Well, I'll be off, then, and find a bed for us.

CINESIAS. Oh! 'tis not worth while; we can lie on the ground surely.

MYRRHINÉ. No, no! bad man as you are, I don't like your lying on the bare earth.

CINESIAS. Ah! how the dear girl loves me!

MYRRHINÉ. [*coming back with a bed.*] Come, get to bed quick; I am going to undress. But, plague take it, we must get a mattress.

CINESIAS. A mattress! Oh! no, never mind!

MYRRHINÉ. No, by Artemis! lie on the bare sacking, never! That were too squalid.

CINESIAS. A kiss!

MYRRHINÉ. Wait a minute!

CINESIAS. Oh! by the great gods, be quick back!

MYRRHINÉ. [*coming back with a mattress.*] Here is a mattress. Lie down, I am just going to undress. But, but you've got no pillow.

CINESIAS. I don't want one, no, no.

MYRRHINÉ. But *I* do.

CINESIAS. Oh! dear, oh, dear! they treat my poor penis for all the world like Heracles.[60]

MYRRHINÉ. [*coming back with a pillow.*] There, lift your head, dear!

CINESIAS. That's really everything.

MYRRHINÉ. Is it everything, I wonder.

CINESIAS. Come, my treasure.

MYRRHINÉ. I am just unfastening my girdle. But remember what you promised me about making Peace; mind you keep your word.

CINESIAS. Yes, yes, upon my life I will.

MYRRHINÉ. Why, you have no blanket.

CINESIAS. Great Zeus! what matter of that? 'tis you I want to fuck.

MYRRHINÉ. Never fear—directly, directly! I'll be back in no time.

---

[59] A spring so named within the precincts of the Acropolis.

[60] The comic poets delighted in introducing Heracles (Hercules) on the stage as an insatiable glutton, whom the other characters were for ever tantalizing by promising toothsome dishes and then making him wait indefinitely for their arrival.

CINESIAS. The woman will kill me with her blankets!

MYRRHINÉ. [*coming back with a blanket.*] Now, get up for one moment.

CINESIAS. But I tell you, our friend here is up—all stiff and ready!

MYRRHINÉ. Would you like me to scent you?

CINESIAS. No, by Apollo, no, please!

MYRRHINÉ. Yes, by Aphrodité, but I will, whether you wish it or no.

CINESIAS. Ah! great Zeus, may she soon be done!

MYRRHINÉ. [*coming back with a flask of perfume.*] Hold out your hand; now rub it in.

CINESIAS. Oh! in Apollo's name, I don't much like the smell of it; but perhaps 'twill improve when it's well rubbed in. It does not somehow smack of the marriage bed!

MYRRHINÉ. There, what a scatterbrain I am; if I have not brought Rhodian perfumes![61]

CINESIAS. Never mind, dearest, let be now.

MYRRHINÉ. You are joking!

CINESIAS. Deuce take the man who first invented perfumes, say I!

MYRRHINÉ. [*coming back with another flask.*] Here, take this bottle.

CINESIAS. I have a better all ready for your service, darling. Come, you provoking creature, to bed with you, and don't bring another thing.

MYRRHINÉ. Coming, coming; I'm just slipping off my shoes. Dear boy, will you vote for peace?

CINESIAS. I'll think about it. [*Myrrhiné runs away.*] I'm a dead man, she is killing me! She has gone, and left me in torment! I must have someone to fuck, I must! Ah me! the loveliest of women has choused and cheated me. Poor little lad (*addressing his penis*), how am I to give you what you want so badly? Where is Cynalopex? quick, man, get him a nurse, do![62]

CHORUS OF OLD MEN. Poor, miserable wretch, baulked in your amorousness! what tortures are yours! Ah! you fill me with pity. Could any man's back and loins stand such a strain? His organ stands stiff and rigid, and there's never a wench to help him!

CINESIAS. Ye gods in heaven, what pains I suffer!

CHORUS OF OLD MEN. Well, there it is; 'tis her doing, that abandoned hussy!

CINESIAS. Nay, nay! rather say that sweetest, dearest darling.

CHORUS OF OLD MEN. That dearest darling? no, no, that hussy, say I! Zeus, thou god of the skies, canst not let loose a hurricane, to sweep them all up into the air, and whirl 'em round, then drop 'em down crash! and impale them on the point of his weapon!

---

[61] The Rhodian perfumes and unguents were less esteemed than the Syrian.

[62] 'Dog-fox,' nickname of a certain notorious Philostratus, keeper of an ATHENIAN brothel of note in Aristophanes' day.

A HEARLD. Say, where shall I find the Senate and the Prytanes? I am bearer of despatches.

MAGISTRATE. But are you a man or a Priapus, pray?[63]

HEARLD. Oh! but he's mighty simple. I am a herald, of course, I swear I am, and I come from Sparta about making peace.

MAGISTRATE. But look, you are hiding a lance under your clothes, surely.

HEARLD. No, nothing of the sort.

MAGISTRATE. Then why do you turn away like that, and hold your cloak out from your body? Have you gotten swellings in the groin with your journey?

HEARLD. By the twin brethren! the man's an old maniac.

MAGISTRATE. Ah, ha! my fine lad, why I can see it standing, oh fie!

HEARLD. I tell you no! but enough of this foolery.

MAGISTRATE. Well, what is it you have there then?

HEARLD. A Lacedaemonian 'skytalé.'[64]

MAGISTRATE. Oh, indeed, a 'skytalé,' is it? Well, well, speak out frankly; I know all about these matters. How are things going at Sparta now?

HEARLD. Why, everything is turned upside down at Sparta; and all the allies are half dead with lusting. We simply must have Pellené.[65]

MAGISTRATE. What is the reason of it all? Is it the god Pan's doing?

HEARLD. No, but Lampito's and the Spartan women's, acting at her instigation; they have denied the men all access to their cunts.

MAGISTRATE. But whatever do you do?

HEARLD. We are at our wits' end; we walk bent double, just as if we were carrying lanterns in a wind. The jades have sworn we shall not so much as touch their cunts till we have all agreed to conclude peace.

MAGISTRATE. Ha, ha! So I see now, 'tis a general conspiracy embracing all Greece. Go you back to Sparta and bid them send Envoys with plenary powers to treat for peace. I will urge our Senators myself to name Plenipotentiaries from us; and to persuade them, why, I will show them this. [*Pointing to his erect penis.*]

HEARLD. What could be better? I fly at your command.

---

[63] The god of gardens—and of lubricity; represented by a grotesque figure with an enormous penis.

[64] A staff in use among the Lacedaemonians for writing cipher despatches. A strip of leather or paper was wound round the 'skytalé,' on which the required message was written lengthwise, so that when unrolled it became unintelligible; the recipient abroad had a staff of the same thickness and pattern, and so was enabled by rewinding the document to decipher the words.

[65] A city of Achaia, the acquisition of which had long been an object of Lacedaemonian ambition. To make the joke intelligible here, we must suppose Pellené was also the name of some notorious courtesan of the day.

CHORUS OF OLD MEN. No wild beast is there, no flame of fire, more fierce and untameable than woman; the panther is less savage and shameless.

CHORUS OF WOMEN. And yet you dare to make war upon me, wretch, when you might have me for your most faithful friend and ally.

CHORUS OF OLD MEN. Never, never can my hatred cease towards women.

CHORUS OF WOMEN. Well, please yourself. Still I cannot bear to leave you all naked as you are; folks would laugh at me. Come, I am going to put this tunic on you.

CHORUS OF OLD MEN. You are right, upon my word! it was only in my confounded fit of rage I took it off.

CHORUS OF WOMEN. Now at any rate you look like a man, and they won't make fun of you. Ah! if you had not offended me so badly, I would take out that nasty insect you have in your eye for you.

CHORUS OF OLD MEN. Ah! so that's what was annoying me so! Look, here's a ring, just remove the insect, and show it me. By Zeus! it has been hurting my eye this ever so long.

CHORUS OF WOMEN. Well, I agree, though your manners are not over and above pleasant. Oh! what a huge great gnat! just look! It's from Tricorysus, for sure.[66]

CHORUS OF OLD MEN. A thousand thanks! the creature was digging a regular well in my eye; now it's gone, my tears flow freely.

CHORUS OF WOMEN. I will wipe them for you—bad, naughty man though you are. Now, just one kiss.

CHORUS OF OLD MEN. No—a kiss, certainly not!

CHORUS OF WOMEN. Just one, whether you like it or not.

CHORUS OF OLD MEN. Oh! those confounded women! how they do cajole us! How true the saying: "'Tis impossible to live with the baggages, impossible to live without 'em"! Come, let us agree for the future not to regard each other any more as enemies; and to clinch the bargain, let us sing a choric song.

CHORUS OF WOMEN. We desire, Athenians, to speak ill of no man; but on the contrary to say much good of everyone, and to *do* the like. We have had enough of misfortunes and calamities. Is there any, man or woman, wants a bit of money—two or three minas or so;[67] well, our purse is full. If only peace is concluded, the borrower will not have to pay back. Also I'm inviting to supper a few Carystian friends,[68] who are excellently well qualified. I have still a drop of

---

[66] A deme of Attica, abounding in woods and marshes, where the gnats were particularly troublesome. There is very likely also an allusion to the spiteful, teasing character of its inhabitants.

[67] A mina was a little over £4; 60 minas made a talent.

[68] Carystus was a city of Euboea notorious for the dissoluteness of its inhabitants; hence the inclusion of these Carystian youths in the women's invitation.

good soup left, and a young porker I'm going to kill, and the flesh
will be sweet and tender. I shall expect you at my house to-day; but
first away to the baths with you, you and your children; then come
all of you, ask no one's leave, but walk straight up, as if you were
at home; never fear, the door will be ... shut in your faces![69]

CHORUS OF OLD MEN. Ah! here come the Envoys from Sparta with
their long flowing beards; why, you would think they wore a
cage[70] between their thighs. [*Enter the Lacedaemonian Envoys.*]
Hail to you, first of all, Laconians; then tell us how you fare.

A LACONIAN. No need for many words; you see what a state we are in.

CHORUS OF OLD MEN. Alas! the situation grows more and more
strained! the intensity of the thing is just frightful.

LACONIAN. 'Tis beyond belief. But to work! summon your
Commissioners, and let us patch up the best peace we may.

CHORUS OF OLD MEN. Ah! our men too, like wrestlers in the arena,
cannot endure a rag over their bellies; 'tis an athlete's malady,
which only exercise can remedy.

AN ATHENIAN. Can anybody tell us where Lysistrata is? Surely she will
have some compassion on our condition.

CHORUS OF OLD MEN. Look! 'tis the very same complaint. [*Addressing
the ATHENIAN.*] Don't you feel of mornings a strong nervous
tension?

ATHENIAN. Yes, and a dreadful, dreadful torture it is! Unless peace is
made very soon, we shall find no resource but to fuck Clisthenes.[71]

CHORUS OF OLD MEN. Take my advice, and put on your clothes again;
one of the fellows who mutilated the Hermae[72] might see you.

ATHENIAN. You are right.

LACONIAN. Quite right. There, I will slip on my tunic.

ATHENIAN. Oh! what a terrible state we are in! Greeting to you,
Laconian fellow-sufferers.

LACONIAN. [*addressing one of his countrymen.*] Ah! my boy, what a
thing it would have been if these fellows had seen us just now
when our tools were on full stand!

ATHENIAN. Speak out, Laconians, what is it brings you here?

LACONIAN. We have come to treat for peace.

ATHENIAN. Well said; we are of the same mind. Better call Lysistrata
then; she is the only person will bring us to terms.

---

[69] A παρὰ προσδοκίαν; *i.e.* exactly the opposite of the word expected is used to
conclude the sentence—to move the sudden hilarity of the audience as a finale to the
scene.

[70] A wattled cage or pen for pigs.

[71] An effeminate, a pathic; failing women, they will have to resort to pederasty.

[72] These *Hermae* were half-length figures of the god Hermes, which stood at the
corners of streets and in public places at Athens. One night, just before the sailing of the
Sicilian Expedition, they were all mutilated—to the consternation of the inhabitants.
Alcibiades and his wild companions were suspected of the outrage.

LACONIAN. Yes, yes—and Lysistratus into the bargain, if you will.

CHORUS OF OLD MEN. Needless to call her; she has heard your voices, and here she comes.

ATHENIAN. Hail, boldest and bravest of womankind! The time is come to show yourself in turn uncompromising and conciliatory, exacting and yielding, haughty and condescending. Call up all your skill and artfulness. Lo! the foremost men in Hellas, seduced by your fascinations, are agreed to entrust you with the task of ending their quarrels.

LYSISTRATA. 'Twill be an easy task—if only they refrain from mutual indulgence in masculine love; if they do, I shall know the fact at once. Now, where is the gentle goddess Peace? Lead hither the Laconian Envoys. But, look you, no roughness or violence; our husbands always behaved so boorishly.[73] Bring them to me with smiles, as women should. If any refuse to give you his hand, then catch him by the penis and draw him politely forward. Bring up the Athenians too; you may take them just how you will. Laconians, approach; and you, Athenians, on my other side. Now hearken all! I am but a woman; but I have good common sense; Nature has dowered me with discriminating judgment, which I have yet further developed, thanks to the wise teachings of my father and the elders of the city. First I must bring a reproach against you that applies equally to both sides. At Olympia, and Thermopylae, and Delphi, and a score of other places too numerous to mention, you celebrate before the same altars ceremonies common to all Hellenes; yet you go cutting each other's throats, and sacking Hellenic cities, when all the while the Barbarian is yonder threatening you! That is my first point.

ATHENIAN. Ah, ah! concupiscence is killing me!

LYSISTRATA. Now 'tis to you I address myself, Laconians. Have you forgotten how Periclides,[74] your own countryman, sat a suppliant before our altars? How pale he was in his purple robes! He had come to crave an army of us; 'twas the time when Messenia was pressing you sore, and the Sea-god was shaking the earth. Cimon marched to your aid at the head of four thousand hoplites, and saved Lacedaemon. And, after such a service as that, you ravage the soil of your benefactors!

ATHENIAN. They do wrong, very wrong, Lysistrata.

---

[73] They had repeatedly dismissed with scant courtesy successive Lacedaemonian embassies coming to propose terms of peace after the notable ATHENIAN successes at Pylos, when the Island of Sphacteria was captured and 600 Spartan citizens brought prisoners to Athens. This was in 425 B.C., the seventh year of the War.

[74] Chief of the Lacedaemonian embassy which came to Athens, after the earthquake of 464 B.C., which almost annihilated the town of Sparta, to invoke the help of the Athenians against the revolted Messenians and helots.

LACONIAN. We do wrong, very wrong. Ah! great gods! what lovely thighs she has!

LYSISTRATA. And now a word to the Athenians. Have you no memory left of how, in the days when ye wore the tunic of slaves, the Laconians came, spear in hand, and slew a host of Thessalians and partisans of Hippias the Tyrant? They, and they only, fought on your side on that eventful day; they delivered you from despotism, and thanks to them our Nation could change the short tunic of the slave for the long cloak of the free man.

LACONIAN. I have never seen a woman of more gracious dignity.

ATHENIAN. I have never seen a woman with a finer cunt!

LYSISTRATA. Bound by such ties of mutual kindness, how can you bear to be at war? Stop, stay the hateful strife, be reconciled; what hinders you?

LACONIAN. We are quite ready, if they will give us back our rampart.

LYSISTRATA. What rampart, my dear man?

LACONIAN. Pylos, which we have been asking for and craving for ever so long.

ATHENIAN. In the Sea-god's name, you shall never have it!

LYSISTRATA. Agree, my friends, agree.

ATHENIAN. But then what city shall we be able to stir up trouble in?

LYSISTRATA. Ask for another place in exchange.

ATHENIAN. Ah! that's the ticket! Well, to begin with, give us Echinus, the Maliac gulf adjoining, and the two legs of Megara.[75]

LACONIAN. Oh! surely, surely not all that, my dear sir.

LYSISTRATA. Come to terms; never make a difficulty of two legs more or less!

ATHENIAN. Well, I'm ready now to off coat and cultivate my land.

LACONIAN. And I too, to dung it to start with.

LYSISTRATA. That's just what you shall do, once peace is signed. So, if you really want to make it, go consult your allies about the matter.

ATHENIAN. What allies, I should like to know? Why, we are *all* on the stand; not one but is mad to be fucking. What we all want, is to be abed with our wives; how should our allies fail to second our project?

LACONIAN. And ours the same, for certain sure!

ATHENIANS. The Carystians first and foremost, by the gods!

LYSISTRATA. Well said, indeed! Now be off to purify yourselves for entering the Acropolis, where the women invite you to supper; we will empty our provision baskets to do you honour. At table, you

---

[75] Echinus was a town on the Thessalian coast, at the entrance to the Maliac Gulf, near Thermopylae and opposite the northern end of the ATHENIAN island of Euboea. By the "legs of Megara" are meant the two "long walls" or lines of fortification connecting the city of Megara with its seaport Nisaea—in the same way as Piraeus was joined to Athens.

will exchange oaths and pledges; then each man will go home with his wife.

ATHENIAN. Come along then, and as quick as may be.

LACONIAN. Lead on; I'm your man.

ATHENIAN. Quick, quick's the word, say I.

CHORUS OF WOMEN. Embroidered stuffs, and dainty tunics, and flowing gowns, and golden ornaments, everything I have, I offer them you with all my heart; take them all for your children, for your girls, against they are chosen "basket-bearers" to the goddess. I invite you every one to enter, come in and choose whatever you will; there is nothing so well fastened, you cannot break the seals, and carry away the contents. Look about you everywhere … you won't find a blessed thing, unless you have sharper eyes than mine.[76] And if any of you lacks corn to feed his slaves and his young and numerous family, why, I have a few grains of wheat at home; let him take what I have to give, a big twelve-pound loaf included. So let my poorer neighbours all come with bags and wallets; my man, Manes, shall give them corn; but I warn them not to come near my door, or—beware the dog![77]

A MARKET-LOUNGER. I say, you, open the door!

A SLAVE. Go your way, I tell you. Why, bless me, they're sitting down now; I shall have to singe 'em with my torch to make 'em stir! What an impudent lot of fellows!

MARKET-LOUNGER. I don't mean to budge.

SLAVE. Well, as you *must* stop, and I don't want to offend you—but you'll see some queer sights.

MARKET-LOUNGER. Well and good, I've no objection.

SLAVE. No, no, you must be off—or I'll tear your hair out, I will; be off, I say, and don't annoy the Laconian Envoys; they're just coming out from the banquet-hall.

AN ATHENIAN. Such a merry banquet I've never seen before! The Laconians were simply charming. After the drink is in, why, we're all wise men, all. It's only natural, to be sure, for sober, we're all fools. Take my advice, my fellow-countrymen, our Envoys should always be drunk. We go to Sparta; we enter the city sober; why, we must be picking a quarrel directly. We don't understand what they say to us, we imagine a lot they don't say at all, and we report home all wrong, all topsy-turvy. But, look you, to-day it's quite different; we're enchanted whatever happens; instead of Clitagoras, they might sing us Telamon,[78] and we should clap our

---

[76] Examples of παρὰ προσδοκίαν again; see above.

[77] Examples of παρὰ προσδοκίαν again; see above.

[78] Clitagoras was a composer of drinking songs, Telamon of war songs.

hands just the same. A perjury or two into the bargain, la! what does that matter to merry companions in their cups?

SLAVE. But here they are back again! Will you begone, you loafing scoundrels.

MARKET-LOUNGER. Ah ha! here's the company coming out already.

A LACONIAN. My dear, sweet friend, come, take your flute in hand; I would fain dance and sing my best in honour of the Athenians and our noble selves.

AN ATHENIAN. Yes, take your flute, i' the gods' name. What a delight to see him dance!

CHORUS OF LACONIANS. Oh Mnemosyné! inspire these men, inspire my muse who knows our exploits and those of the Athenians. With what a godlike ardour did they swoop down at Artemisium[79] on the ships of the Medes! What a glorious victory was that! For the soldiers of Leonidas,[80] they were like fierce wild-boars whetting their tushes. The sweat ran down their faces, and drenched all their limbs, for verily the Persians were as many as the sands of the seashore. Oh! Artemis, huntress queen, whose arrows pierce the denizens of the woods, virgin goddess, be thou favourable to the Peace we here conclude; through thee may our hearts be long united! May this treaty draw close for ever the bonds of a happy friendship! No more wiles and stratagems! Aid us, oh! aid us, maiden huntress!

LYSISTRATA. All is for the best; and now, Laconians, take your wives away home with you, and you, Athenians, yours. May husband live happily with wife, and wife with husband. Dance, dance, to celebrate our bliss, and let us be heedful to avoid like mistakes for the future.

CHORUS OF ATHENIANS Appear, appear, dancers, and the Graces with you! Let us invoke, one and all, Artemis, and her heavenly brother, gracious Apollo, patron of the dance, and Dionysus, whose eye darts flame, as he steps forward surrounded by the Maenad maids, and Zeus, who wields the flashing lightning, and his august, thrice-blessed spouse, the Queen of Heaven! These let us invoke, and all the other gods, calling all the inhabitants of the skies to witness the noble Peace now concluded under the fond auspices of Aphrodité. Io Paean! Io Paean! dance, leap, as in honour of a victory won. Evoé! Evoé! And you, our Laconian guests, sing us a new and inspiring strain!

CHORUS OF LACONIANS. Leave once more, oh! leave once more the noble height of Taygetus, oh! Muse of Lacedaemon, and join us in

---

[79] Here, off the north coast of Euboea, the Greeks defeated the Persians in a naval battle, 480 B.C.

[80] The hero of Thermopylae, where the 300 Athenians arrested the advance of the invading hosts of Xerxes in the same year.

singing the praises of Apollo of Amyclae, and Athena of the Brazen House, and the gallant twin sons of Tyndarus, who practise arms on the banks of Eurotas river.[81] Haste, haste hither with nimble-footed pace, let us sing Sparta, the city that delights in choruses divinely sweet and graceful dances, when our maidens bound lightly by the river side, like frolicsome fillies, beating the ground with rapid steps and shaking their long locks in the wind, as Bacchantes wave their wands in the wild revels of the Wine-god. At their head, oh! chaste and beauteous goddess, daughter of Latona, Artemis, do thou lead the song and dance. A fillet binding thy waving tresses, appear in thy loveliness; leap like a fawn; strike thy divine hands together to animate the dance, and aid us to renown the valiant goddess of battles, great Athené of the Brazen House!

THE END

---

[81] Amyclae, an ancient town on the Eurotas within two or three miles of Sparta, the traditional birthplace of Castor and Pollux; here stood a famous and magnificent Temple of Apollo.

"Of the Brazen House," a surname of Athené, from the Temple dedicated to her worship at Chalcis in Euboea, the walls of which were covered with plates of brass.

Sons of Tyndarus, that is, Castor and Pollux, "the great twin brethren," held in peculiar reverence at Sparta.

15291852R00026

Made in the USA
Middletown, DE
21 November 2018